THE JEW AND THE CROSS

DAGOBERT D. RUNES

the
Jew
and
the
CROSS

PHILOSOPHICAL LIBRARY   New York

God can not hate
nor does He punish.

—BARUCH SPINOZA

Contents

Contents

THE JEW AND THE CROSS

I

The Bishops of Rome

This is going to be a small book, dealing with a large subject. I do not think it necessary to burden the reader with statistics, quotations and bibliographical references. The facts in the matter speak for themselves.

The issue at hand is simply: Jew hatred, or, to use the Germanic nineteenth century term, anti-Semitism. I do not desire to add another sociological study of this much belabored topic. What compels me to write is the unavoidable melancholic truth that there is such an issue. It is very much alive, and no less than at its beginning in the early centuries of Christianity.

Anti-Semitism was born with Christianity; to be sure, not with Jesus, a Jew Himself, whose followers took conviction in his descendancy from the House of David, but rather with those who, on the basis of the sermons flowing from the lips of the gentle Nazarene, created an organized church with priests, deacons, bishops and vestrymen.

This rapidly spreading religious body, dedicated to the gospel of Christ, in due process of multiple revisions formulated a New Testament for the guidance of its followers, teachers, and clergy, and gave it a final version in the 4th century which dramatized in a most touching manner the life and self-willed death of Jeshu Ben Joseph, in which drama, however, the Jew was assigned, with a cold and merciless gesture, the image of the devil himself.

The four writers of the church whose works we have only in the Greek script of the 4th century, the era in which the pagan king Constantine turned over the shrines and temples of manifold faiths of the Roman Empire to the Christian Bishop of Rome, made it reverently clear that all the people of the world, being offspring of sinful Adam, exiled from the paradise, be therefore by mere birth creatures of the original sin, congenitally enchained by lust, greed, and debauchery.

The only person exempt from the original sin is the Holy Mother. But God sent His only begotten son to this earth, and taking upon Himself the suffering and torture of crucifixion, Christ redeemed believing mankind. Such is the compassion of the Lord, such is the nature of the Holy Spirit, and such is the blessing of Christianity.

The writers of the Catholic Church were given directions

to separate the people of Israel, Christ's very own people, from the other so-called non-believers. They changed the self-willed death of the redeemer into a case of a judicial murder on the part of a Jewish "people's court." They wrote in one scene of their sacred play that the Lord wanted to die, thus taking the original sin of mankind upon Himself. In another scene they made the Lord a pitiful victim of vicious Jewish zealots, making not only the Jews of Jerusalem responsible for this alleged assassination by a Judeo-Roman court, but also the millions of Jews of that time who lived in Alexandria, in Babylon and elsewhere, and who had neither part nor knowledge of the events in the Holy Land. The scribes of the church further made responsible the Jews of all future generations. At this very writing there are Catholic cardinals, bishops and priests meeting in Rome, some of whom still insist that the Jews of today must share the responsibility for the death of Christ.

In this light, the bizarre request of a loud Greek Orthodox Christian may not be found ludicrous; he suggested that not only the Jews of the post-Christian era, but all the Jews of the pre-Christian era, including the prophets, the kings of Israel, and Moses and Abraham, be judged perfidious participants in the latter day crucifixion. The learned clergyman desired to make a complete chain of condemnation around the Jewish people, embracing tomorrow as well as yesterday.

If Jesus was God, if we accept Christian theology, then His death was self-ordained, was providential, the great act of redemption of a sinful people.

13

To accuse His people of carrying the guilt of the crucifixion is reducing Christ to a mere dreamer, a preacher, a
sectarian.

The Holy Land at the time of Jesus was seething with
foreigners and visitors from all parts of the Roman Empire.
By the very records of the scribes of the New Testament,
only the Jews hearkened to the Redeemer, only Jews did
He select as His apostles, and it was a Jew, Saul of Tarsus,
who, after the death of Christ, finally became the builder of
the church.

Christ became a Jew by circumcision, as He was born
from the womb of a Jewish woman. His kin and friends
were Jews. He lived the life of a Son of Israel, celebrated the
great holidays of His nation and mourned with them on the
memorial days of their tragedies.

Those who listened to His Sermon on the Mount were
Jews, those who traveled with Him to Jerusalem were Jews,
and those who mourned His death were Jews. Spiritual
Christianity while Christ was alive on earth was all Jewish.
The preachers of the gospels, when the voice of Christ was
still lingering in the ears and the hearts of his contemporaries, were all Jewish. What we find of them in the 4th
century was no longer Jewish, but it was also no longer of
Christ.

The bishops of Rome, with the help of Roman Imper-
ators, had taken Christianity, its churches and its responsi-
bilities, its doctrines and its theology, to a cold and calcu-
lating bosom.

A new era began, the era of Christianity not as the solemn teachings of a gentle Jew, but as a powerful body of

14

involved edicts, codes and doctrines that affected the whole Western world. The nations of the Roman Empire, without leadership and broken in spirit, submitted to the wishes of the Bishop of Rome, all except the Jews. The Jew would not surrender, neither in Judea nor in Egypt, neither in Persia nor in Libya. Not even in Rome.

So the Bishop of Rome, who in the 4th century became the master of the souls of Europe, put the mark of perfidy on the name and title of every Jew in his realm and elsewhere. And this blot he willed should remain upon the children and children's children of the House of Israel; and because of this stigma, for more than 1500 years Christians have always found it easy to deal with Jews as non-beings. *Judai monstra sunt.*

It was the Bishop of Rome who in the 13th century directed that the blot which was placed upon the Jew should also be carried on his clothing, visible to all.

It was the Bishop of Rome who ordered in the 15th century that the marked people be confined to ghettos so that they might not soil the Christians around them.

It was the Bishop of Rome who used the Crusades against the Moslems as an occasion to heap blemish upon the Jews.

It was the Bishop of Rome who was the spiritual head of the *auto-da-fé,* in which in Spain alone nine thousand Jewish patricians were burned *ad majorem Christi gloriam.* And in our time, it was the Bishop of Rome who refused to utter a single sentence of horror, nay, disapproval, of the choking to death by German Christians of one million Jewish children and five million Jewish women and unarmed men.

15

We Jews have all the records of those of our nation who were massacred in the places where Christianity held forth. Our books of tears and our books of blood are multiple, and we are a now small people, cast upon the rock of Judaism in an ocean of Christianity.

They killed my mother, holding her responsible for the death of Christ. She had committed no crime except that she was of the same blood as Christ himself. Even my two-year-old grandson already has upon him their mark as being a Christ killer, by the mere fact of being a Jew.

While many Jews in ancient Israel accepted Christ, others did not. Neither did the Greeks nor Parthians, the Romans nor Arabs; neither did members of Christ's own family and friends. Neither did Jesus' father accept Him as the Messiah.

And what became of the undoubtedly great family in which Jesus grew up, what became of the many relatives of His father, His mother, and the friends He lived with? They lived on as Jews, until somewhere along the line, traveling through the centuries of a Christian Europe, they were set upon by those who called themselves after the Redeemer, and put to disgrace or to torture and death.

How many descendants of Christ's own family and friends were victim to the crusading adventurers sacking the Jewish quarters of Mainz? How many were put to the torch by the Inquisition? And how many were gassed in Hitler Germany?

Perhaps Christ had come to earth to help His people in the many hours of despair and persecution. He may have been among them again and again, trying to protect His

16

brethren, the old, the weak, and the children, and they put Him to death again and again, together with the rest of His people.

Perhaps the Jews in ancient days had martyred one of their own. Perhaps, but this is for certain: the Christians have martyred ten million Jews, and still they do not say, "We shall do it no more. We shall make an end to this calumny and this villainy."

Sometimes they speak sweet words of love and charity, but these are evening words, in the parlor or in public lectures. But their morning words, from the pulpit and in the Sunday schools, are words of hate and words of contempt. In the morning they teach the young, the very young, even before their first communion, the evil message *pro paganos* that the Jews killed poor Lord Christ. You can imagine how a six- or seven-year-old feels the first time the touching tale is related to him of the young Jesus, the gentle preacher, the ever-loving Son of God, with Whom soon every child identifies itself as a divine father figure,—and now came the Jews, who defiled Him and made the Romans arrest Him, who drove nails through His hands and feet, and so cruelly killed Him.

The impact of this monstrous anti-Semitic tale upon the child is indescribable. No matter what you tell the child a decade or two later, this first impression of horror will never leave his or her mind. To those so indoctrinated, the Jew will forever, certainly in their hearts, remain a negative symbol, a non-being, Beelzebub incarnate.

It is true that some exceptionally analytical minds can in later years overcome even the deepest emotionally grounded prejudices of childhood. But the majority are far from being exceptionally analytical minds.

Throughout the history of western Europe, we find evidence of the ease with which dictators or corrupt clerics could sway the minds of the Christians to perpetrate unspeakable crimes upon their Jewish neighbors. As long as the churches, and I mean the Protestant as well as the Catholic, continue to teach the canard of the Jews murdering Christ as gospel truth, every new generation of Christians so raised in hate and derision will be emotionally prepared for active anti-Semitism.

We have no evidence of any murderous misdeed of the Jews against Jesus except the 4th century edition of the gospels written by the scribes of the Bishop of Rome, to the almost total exclusion of all other publications, which in that century were obliterated by the dominant church. We do know, on the other hand, that Jesus himself was a true and believing Jew, as were all His apostles and His early followers. The makers of Christianity were Jews from end to end, and from its beginning, the Jews were the makers of Christianity, not its destroyers. But the Christians have thus far been merciless destroyers of the Jews. We do not know who instigated the death of Jesus, as we do not know anything at all about the last years of Saint Paul, although the church has always decided to blame the death of both on the Jews. This is traditional with them. But if Christ is God, no Jew, nor Roman, could put Him to death. The Christian doctrine teaches that the death of Christ was self-willed, and this very same doctrine excludes the possibility of execution by Jewish instigation.

If the Christians are serious in their declaration and wish to make an end to religious Jew hatred, they have to stop teaching it to the young, and they have to stop preaching it to the old. And while they are busy with this task, let them examine their textbooks, their hymnals, and their prayer-books, and extirpate honestly and sincerely all those gratu-itous, libelous remarks about the Jews, their nefariousness, their perfidy, and their accursedness. There really is no need, in a prayer to Holy Mother Mary, to refer to her peo-ple as the "brood of the devil."

If the Christians wish truly to make amends and are honest in repenting their historic and their theological er-rors, they will have to break tradition. Such tradition as they must abandon however is not of divine heritage, but rather bred by hate and cunning. God loved the Jews and chose them as His people, and therefore His only son was born into those people, and if you love Christ, you cannot hold His people in infamy.

II

Reconciliation and Slander

There is a tendency among many Jewish historians and theologians to tread gently upon the sensitive grounds of Christian church history. I do not wish to needlessly offend the faith, rituals or even customs of the Gentiles. But I will not play deaf or dumb and look the other way when slanderous, deadly malice is heaped upon my people. Let us call a spade a spade, especially when we find it in the hands of our gravediggers; and I am not speaking metaphorically.

I do not wish even to elaborate on the sad history of Vaticanism. That has been done to the rim by the various Protestant sects. Nor do I wish to brighten the pages of this small book with the abundantly available satirical barrels of repartée supplied by an enraged Catholic clergy on the subject of obscene vulgarity and plain obscenity of Protestant denominations.

My concern here rests with the attitude and activity of the Christian churches in relation to the Jewish people.

Some liberal Protestant ministers of this and the last century have on occasion veered away so far from the anti-Semitism common to the Christian doctrine that they rose to make public appeals to the Jews, asking for better understanding of Christianity. They put the Jews, so to say, right in the church aisle and demanded, "Why don't you learn more about our Lord Jesus and the meaning of our teachings?"

Such frank appeal for reconciliation of the faiths appears at first glance as attractive as it seems inviting.

On occasion there is even formation of groups, clubs and associations for the betterment of religious relations. This is all very pretty, pleasant and nice at evening bazaars or evening lecture meetings.

However, the very same tolerant and quite tolerable ministers, and even some priests, send out in their Sunday schools and morning services the ugly tale of alleged Jerusalem assassins dramatically presented by the scribes of the Bishop of Rome and philosophically elaborated on by the whole body of early church fathers from Origen to Eusebius, Jerome, Cyril, Augustinus, Athanasius, Cyprian, Ambrose, up to King Constantine, the pagan founder of Catholic supremacy, killer of his wife and killer of his son.

Why should we be gentle about these beatified and canonized spiritual founders of Christian anti-Semitism?

Those who know church history are aware that the early Church Fathers heaped the worst possible abuse upon the people of Israel, the people in whose very bosom were born not only Lord Jesus but all those that were living in fellowship with Christ. They attributed to them all evil in the world, no matter where it occurred, in Cathay or in Brittany, in Ethiopia or in Armenia, in Iberia or even in Atlantis. All poison, venom, grief, sin and corruption, were put at the feet of the Jews by these fanatical men of libelous letters. And Constantine added, only the Lord knows why, that the synagogues were no better than bordellos.

I should like to insert here that no rabbinate or temple ever kept a bordello, but there are pages in the history of the Papacy where such are implied at the banks of the Tiber.

There is no need for liberal preachers, either of the Protestant or of the Catholic vintage, to teach the Jew understanding of Christianity. We have been taught lessons in Christianity for almost two thousand years.

The streets of Seville, of Toledo, of Cordova and Madrid, of Lisbon and Paris, of York, of Rome, of Worms and Vienna, of Dachau and Belsen, of Warsaw, and of Holy Jerusalem itself, where the Crusaders burned every living Jew as a symbol of liberation—all these and a thousand places more are overwhelming evidence of what Christianity is like in action.

We understand Christianity. We do not always express the horror in our hearts, because we feel the faith of the believer is a holy thing.

I do not feel that way. I feel that some aspects of the Christian faith, and I refer again to the horror Gospel of Jewish assassinism, are pernicious, inhuman and totally unfounded.

And even if it were true that all the people in ancient Palestine worshiped the advent of Jesus as the coming of the Messiah, whom certainly the pagans did not expect, and that of all people the Jews turned their backs on Him, and that all His apostles were Romans like the reigning popes to come, and that Paulus was a Persian, even if all that were so, and if those disbelieving Jews saw in Jesus no more than an impostor and put Him to death by themselves, as has been done to a thousand prophets in a thousand instances all over this most imperfect globe, is it not time to make an end to persecuting the living of today for a death two thousand years ago? And if Jesus was God, and I do not say He was not, how could man kill God? And if God took upon Himself the cross of death and is resurrected in the heavens, and I do not say He is not, why then blame the Jews for a death that never was, when the life is there for ever and ever?

The pope is there in Rome, as the one before him and the one before that, and they pride themselves on their Roman blood. Do Christians vilify them because their ancestors put Christ to death? But the pope reigning today, Paulus VI, in this year's Easter message found it necessary to beatify his Easter sermon for peace by the rhetorical outrage that the perfidious Jews had insulted the Lord Jesus, scourged, and finally murdered Him. Thus spoke the pope in a message of peace.

24

23123

I know that some Protestants of the left wing, those who
have strayed so far away from the Gospel that they rarely
quote the Scripture, but mostly each other, hate to go back
to the Book, it is so fundamentalistic and often embarrassing. But let me remind you what the undisputed leader of
Protestantism has wished upon the Jews. This is Martin
Luther I am now quoting, who became a monk and a priest
in his flight from Satan. This is what Martin Luther gath-
ered from studying the Scripture as set down by the evan-
gelists of the Bishop of Rome in the fourth century. He
called the Jews a "damned, rejected race." The only way for
Christians to deal with the Jews is to

> "Set their synagogues on fire, and whatever does not
> burn up should be covered or spread over with dirt
> so that no one may ever be able to see a cinder or stone
> of it . . . in order that God may see that we are Chris-
> tians. . . . Their homes should likewise be broken down
> and destroyed. . . . They should be put under one roof
> or in a stable, like gypsies, in order that they may re-
> alize that they are not masters in our land, as they
> boast, but miserable captives, as they complain of us
> incessantly before God with bitter wailing. . . . They
> should be deprived of their prayer books and Tal-
> muds, in which such idolatry, lies, cursing, and blas-
> phemy are taught . . . their rabbis must be forbidden
> to teach under the threat of death."

It is only natural that such fountainhead of German
Protestantism would spread the seed of Hitlerism in all its
savagery and bestiality.

25

Christianity is beset by a hundred heresies but there is one issue which is fundamental to all of them, be they Greek Orthodox or Anglican, Presbyterian or Baptist, Lutheran or Roman: the Jew be damned.

The Gospel version of the Jesus trial, as presented to us by the scribes of the Bishop of Rome as the great judicial event of the first century, is terrifying in its cunning malevolence:

Pontius Pilatus, a fellow Roman, and the chief legal authority, pitifully pleading for the release of Jesus, an upright and innocent man, and the "God"-hating Jewish court mob clamoring for the death of God, yelling out: If he is innocent his blood be on us and on our children.

By relating this completely unrealistic trial in this manner the scribes of the Bishop of Rome have thus achieved two ends. First, to make out of the Roman savage conquerors and masters of world-wide destruction a symbol of pure innocence and justice, while on the other hand marking the whole Jewish nation assassins of God who, by their own demand, have turned the curse of God upon themselves forever.

While whitewashing their countrymen, the Bishops of Rome so blackened the Jews that all generations of Christians to come would find the Jew the outcast upon whom the exercise of the most cruel bestiality could only be considered a just punishment of vengeful God. And if God in his ire could use Vespasian and Titus to kill, maim and disperse, then perhaps He could have used Adolf Hitler to mete out justice upon this forever accursed people.

As the doctrine of Catholicism stands today, every Jew alive is damned as being congenitally the murderer of God. Such are also the teachings of the Greek Orthodox Church.

Some of the Protestant sects adhere to this concept of early fundamentalism. Others have found various evasive doctrinal formulations, in all of which, however, the Jew remains the killer of God. To give evidence of their new-won tolerance they are making strenuous efforts to push the Jewish crime into the background of antiquity, and some of them even manage to avoid speaking of the gallows in the house of the murderer. They mean to be magnanimous and subtle, but we Jews feel like the innocent who has been forgiven a crime he never committed. And we thoroughly resent and reject such Christian forgiveness, as we resent the brutal primitiveness of the cardinal of Messina who insists that our infants are forever damned as offspring of crucifiers.

We want none of this charity and none of this malicious slander. We want Christianity to cleanse itself of the unhistoric and false notion regarding the Messianic symbol of death and resurrection.

We have made Christianity in all its beauty and Hebraic wisdom. As Jesus said, "I came to fulfill the Torah of Moses and not to destroy it." We were the vessel of the essence of Christianity at a time when the ancestors of the popes were throwing captives to the lions in Rome, and the ancestors of Luther were drinking the blood of their enemies. It is time for Christianity to redeem itself from the heresy of deadly malice against the very descendants of apostolic Christendom.

27

III

Dialogue and Deicide

At the beginning of the Christian era, for centuries before and centuries after, the Jews were accustomed to true
as well as false prophets. A hundred years after Jesus, the
militant Bar Kochba was proclaimed the Messiah, believed
by some, disbelieved by many, proclaimed by a few,
scorned by the more sophisticated, and ignored by the
masses of the people.

The appearance of Jesus could not have aroused any
great excitement in a land that was seething with unrest,
rebellion and ecstatic religious fervor.

The teachings of the Essenes, the flaming sermons of

the Samaritans, the magic performances of foreign fakirs, the starry-eyed devotionalism of rabbinical followers, the furtive agitation of anti-Roman schemers, the fantastic pronouncements of pre-Kabbalistic mystics—in all this spiritual and social turmoil the solemn figure of the gentle, peripatetic rabbi of Nazareth would arouse little attention and certainly no wild resentment as depicted in the Vatican editions of the fourth century Gospels and Acts.

The people of Israel of the first century were not in the habit of killing dreamers of their own faith. And there is not a single sentence even in the Roman Gospels that can be seriously taken as words of Christ that contradicts or opposes the Mosaic faith. No sober exegete ever denied that Jesus was an upstanding Jew, and an observing Jew, and a most faithful adherent to the Law which was His tradition, the tradition of His father and the tradition of His mother, and that of His whole wide family.

It is true that Jesus emphasized His message and His calling. While it did not always hearken to the voice of prophets who forever claimed to speak the voice of the Lord, Israel did not put its prophets to the gallows.

Not a single man in Israel was ever crucified when the people of Israel, its judges and its priests, dealt with all religious offenses by themselves in their own judicial power.

There is no record of a single case in the whole rich and well-known history of the ancient Jewish people where crucifixion was ever used or urged upon an occupying military force.

On the other hand, crucifixion in the manner described in the Gospels was obligatory penalty for sorcery and high treason in the Roman Empire. Rebellious slaves as well as blasphemous rebels against the state religion were put to the cross in the Roman Empire time and time again.

To many Jews, Jesus was no more than a gentle dreamer calling for spiritual awakening, another dramatic religious hope for the Messianic panacea.

To the Romans, He was an offensive usurper Who called Himself King of the Jews and refused to accept the reigning Caesar as the supreme deity of the land. And they put Him to death as they did many others who refused to bow, pray and burn myrrh before the statue of the Emperor.

The Jews were respected by the Roman Senate and the patricians and equites because of their knowledge, their training and industrial abilities, and because of that, the Mosaic faith was considered *religio licita.* The Romans could never understand why the Jews would worship a god who had no face and no name. The Roman writers ridiculed such unbelievable naïveté and overlooked the indifference of the Jews toward public religious functions of the Roman state, which invariably centered upon the figure of the reigning Caesar.

As the Jews did not put up a visible god or otherwise identifiable divinities in opposition to the great hierarchy dominating the Roman temples, they were the only disbelievers permitted to carry on their services.

Even the synagogues of the Jews were barren of statues or paintings depicting deities. The Jews had no gods of water or fire, the winds or the underworld, no Olympians and no half gods. And even their religious rituals were of a dull, agricultural and dietary character.

The Romans made great efforts to appease Jewish political rebellion and were most generous in granting Roman citizenship with all its privileges to an unusually large number of those of the Hebrew faith.

But the advent of Jesus and His apostles brought into the fore a visible god, a walking and talking god who performed great miracles, and that is something which made Christianity from its inception *religio illicita,* and in such cases the Romans were most severe in the application of the death penalty by crucifixion for the *honesdiores,* and death at the jaws of the beasts for the *humiliores.*

Christianity was directly and competitively offensive to the priests of the divine Caesars, and for three hundred years its members and the witnesses for that faith were martyred by the Emperors of Rome. The word "martyr" means witness.

The witnesses for Christ died the most horrible deaths at the cross and the torch and in the arena, for being inimical to the Roman state religion, until in the early part of the fourth century the ambitious Constantine I, endeavoring to get control over the whole empire and realizing the tremendous power of secretive Christianity, changed the very structure of Europe by making the despised and persecuted the sole and dominant custodians of the faith of all people of the Roman empire. With one stroke he gave the Vatican a power that was to lie heavy over the hearts and heads of Europe for over a thousand years.

All temples and shrines of the Roman pagan world were destroyed practically overnight. Statues of pagan gods were decapitated, buried or thrown into the bay. Of the temples little was left but the pillars, and the few that we have retained intact were saved simply because someone quickly turned them into Christian churches.

The citizens of Rome, as well as the many subject and vassal states, accepted this change, as they were accustomed to accept all edicts bearing the seal of the Emperor or the stamp of the corrupt senate.

The whole Roman world put up the cross at church and at home. All but the Jews. And at that particular time the Vatican decided to write its own history of the life, the suffering and the death of Christ by making the Jews instead of the Romans His executioners.

And that is why until today the millions of Christians to whom the New Testament is history and guidance read into their hearts and minds the false legend of the crucifixion of the Jew Jesus by His own kinsmen. And instead of hating—if there should be hate at all—the Roman popes and cardinals for descending from Christ killers, in their ignorance and mal-instruction they heap scorn and hate upon the Jewish people, who have committed no crime except being of the same blood as the Savior.

Representing the official church of the Roman Empire, the Vatican was eager at the time it came to supreme power to destroy all writings and engravings that would run contrary to the kind of history they wanted to be told. Hundreds of thousands of scrolls and tablets, parchments and

33

folios were burned or buried to make their schemes appear true and make the truth vanish.

And how successful they were, with the help of the many scribes they could muster to write according to their plans and to rewrite what contradicted them. And thus they succeeded in making Christ's own people, His brethren and other kin, His cousins and His neighbors, appear as devilish assassins and the Romans reluctant executioners of Hebraic deviltry.

The fact is that for three hundred years the Romans crucified the Christians. They threw them to the lions and tied them to burning torches.

No right-thinking man will blame those of Italian birth for these many cruelties acted out by their ancestors upon Christ and His followers. Still, the descendants of the very perpetrators of the outrages have managed by sinister theology and misconstrued historiography to make the Jew of all times carry an indelible guilt for a crime he never committed. The execution of Christ was only one of many thousands of such executions of Christian followers by the Roman authorities. It was not a single event, it was not even a rare event. It was a frequent event, and Christian martyrs by the thousands filled the Roman dungeons, the Roman galleys, the Roman penal mines, the Roman circuses of savage bestiality and the Roman crucifixions.

Why blame the Jews, who kept no dungeons, who used no galley slaves, who had no penal mines, who kept no beasts to devour prisoners? Nor did they ever crucify a single man or woman. It is time that history be rectified, not for the sake of the word, or a past long gone by, but for the sake of justice that has been miscarried to the detriment of Christ's own people. I am not speaking against Christianity, but for it. We do not wish to accept Christ as God, but neither do we wish to see the Jews defamed as killers of Christ. There is no dialogue necessary between Christians and Jews. All we wish is the pontifical monologue to stop accusing the Jews of deicide.

IV

The Blessings of the Fathers

It is, of course, difficult to write of such men as the early Church Fathers with that frank directness one can employ in dealing with historic figures whose pictures one is accustomed to see without halos around their heads.

While this halo surrounding the early Church Fathers did inspire a great number of followers of the Christian faith to piety or intense religious observance, to the Jews that halo emanated only a flame of hatred, and in a thousand cases, nay, in a thousand times thousand cases, this is to be taken literally.

The Church Fathers were not sophisticated scholars and

historians, and were ready to accept the elaborate tale of crucifixion as printed and otherwise publicized in the early versions of the Synoptics and soundly Jew-hating John, as well as the mass of letters from the pen of the irrepressible Paulus. Himself a renegade of Judaism, after his lightning conversion he quickly turned from a witness, or martyr, of Judaism to a relentless apostle of Judeo-Christianity.

After Paulus' turning away from and against his own people, not only theologically but also racially, the burden of the new Christian edifice quickly and emphatically turned from the shoulders of the early Judeo-Christians to the pagan and Roman Christians, who found it most practical to look upon Jesus not as another prophetic or heretic figure of Israel but rather as a god of the Roman world whom the sinister Jews assassinated. Within decades the very people of Jesus, Mary and Joseph became anathema. The true history of the growth and life of early Judeo-Christianity was pushed into darkness and a set of fantastic legends became Gospel Truth in all their animosity against the very people of Jeshu Ben Joseph.

The early Church Fathers were complicated theologians: circumspect in this new Christian theology that spread like wildfire to the lowly people of the Roman Empire; broken by scores of dissident sects and mutual accusations of heresy, united not even by the concept of trinity; imbued, however, by one profound emotion: insatiable, violent and pitiless hate against the accursed People of the Book.

Let's see what some of the benimbused saints have to say of the Lord's chosen people. Justin Martyr, who was executed in Rome in 167, for his Christian beliefs, in his appeal to Marcus Aurelius accused the Jews of inciting the Romans to kill the Christians after they had murdered God. In his "Dialogue with Trypho" he wishes that the country of the Jews be rendered a desert and their towns be consumed by flames, that their enemies may eat the fruit of Israel, and that no Jew ever be able to go to Jerusalem.

Another Christian theologian, martyred by the Romans in 251, was Saint Origen, who contended that the Jews were always envious of the Christians and would never cease to lure their unwary neighbors into their net and destroy those who would oppose their evil designs. In fact, whenever fortune turned away from the Christians such could be traced to the Jews.

Another great and erudite theologian, Eusebius, Bishop of Caesarea, who flourished around 300, maintained steadfastly that the Jews of every community would crucify a Christian at the Purim festival every single year as a public demonstration of their feeling against Jesus. Eusebius further asserted that in the Roman-Persian War the Jews purchased ninety thousand Christian prisoners for the mere pleasure of killing them. This kindly saint at the Council of Nicaea was one of the most powerful architects of Christian dogma. He is also the author of the great ecclesiastical history which is the only source of information for much of that era.

Saint Hilary of Poitiers, (died 367), interpreted historically the Jews as a perverse people, forever accursed by God. Saint Ephraem, (died 373), who is held in highest regard by Syrian and other Eastern churches, is the author of a great body of liturgical hymns, a number of which carry maligning references to the Jews, including referring to their synagogues as whorehouses.

Saint Zeno, of the fourth century, Bishop and patron saint of Verona, bewailed the fact that when inspired monks invaded Jewish homes to save Holy Scriptures and in this process killed resisting Jews, only the bones of the dead ones were burned to ashes while there were still many Jews about who could have been burned for the glory of the Lord.

Saint Cyril, Patriarch of Alexandria, (died 444), a noted dogmatist, gave the Jews a choice of exile or conversion. Those who resisted, including the prefect, were stoned to death.

Saint Jerome (died 420), the editor of the Latin *vulgata* and a dictionary of Christian biographies, "proves" in his "Tractatus Against the Jews" that the Jews are incapable of understanding Holy Scripture and that their lies are driving Christians into heresy. They should therefore be most severely prosecuted until they confess to the true faith. He and Saint Augustine could rightly be called the spiritual fathers of the Medieval Inquisition.

Saint Augustine (died 430), Bishop of Hippo and by far the most influential man in Christian theology, called Judaism a corruption. "The true image of the Hebrew is Judas Iscariot, who sells the Lord for silver. The Jew can never spiritually understand the Scriptures and forever will bear the guilt for the death of Jesus because their fathers killed the Savior."

In the eyes of Saint Augustine, the Jews called upon

themselves for all eternity the divine malediction and must serve in no other capacity than as slaves.

Martin Luther, who was much inspired by Saint Augustine, went him one better by demanding that the Jews be made slaves of the slaves, because if they were to be merely slaves they would have some contact with German Christians. Saint Thomas Aquinas (died 1274), a member of the Dominican Order that had the distinction of being a pillar of the Inquisition, philosophized, "It would be perfectly licit to hold the Jews, because of their crucifying the Lord, in perpetual servitude."

Saint Ambrose, a fourth century bishop of Milan, one of the four Latin doctors of the church, a standard bearer of Christian ethics, reprimanded Emperor Theodosius, who ordered the rebuilding of a synagogue in Mesopotamia that had been destroyed at the instigation of a rabid monk. In fact he himself offered to burn the synagogue in Milan, if it hadn't been burned already.

Saint Athanasius, a fourth century bishop of Alexandria, who was honored as the father of orthodoxy, kept insisting that Rome deal with the Jews by use of the sword and that tolerance was no better than treason against Christ.

Saint Cyprian, a third century bishop of Carthage, the most outstanding churchman of that century, executed by the Romans, demanded that the Jews be driven from the land at the point of the sword.

Many of the princes of Christian Europe for a thousand years and more took the precepts of these learned theologians to heart, treating the Jews of their realm as private chattel, using them for their often sordid and exploitative purposes, and when discovery threatened, they sacrificed the Jews to the mob.

The mobs of Europe, as well as their semi-literate clergy, grew up in anti-Semitism. They were baptized not into the loving spirituality of Jesus the Hebrew but into the venomous and carnal animosity of Jew hatred. Nine out of ten Christians prior to the eighteenth century were totally illiterate. The small minority of thinking people could not reach them, but the priests and ministers had their ear every Sunday of every week and every month of every year.

Every visit to a Christian church became then, as it still often becomes today, a journey to the school of contempt. The Jew was perfidious because he would not accept a visible God. The Jew was nefarious because he held on to the belief that the Lord is one and the Lord is justice and the Lord is charity and the Lord is mercy, and there is no god but the God of eternity. In fact if He has a name it is Elohim, *Eternities*. The Jews were accursed, they preached in the churches, as they still do, because as the "Gospel Truth" reads, some of them some thousands of years ago somewhere in Asia put God to death. What blasphemy all this is!

And for two thousand years, the mobs were ever ready to bleed the Jews, to club the Jews, to burn the Jews. The cardinals did it, the princes did it, why not the lowly people?

The early Christian Fathers may have been involved cogitators in theology and metaphysics, but to the Jews they carry no halo. They carry the singe of hatred at the tip of their tongue and pen.

Shall we praise the assassins of our children, shall we glorify the spiritual fathers of the massacres of our ancestors, and shall we indulge in respectful reverence towards those dark men who twisted the cross into daggers against our nation?

We have no quarrel with the great message of Jesus, born out of the prophetic wisdom that lived in the Israel of His time. But we can have no dialogue with the false and hateful adherents of churches who have for two thousand years used the death of a shining Son of Israel to wound and maim, to cut and burn and choke to death the children of His very brethren.

The Vatican has chosen to beatify, to canonize and sanctify the bones of what they call the Fathers of the Church, the illustrious doctors of the faith.

I say, *unum habetis doctorem,* there is only one Rabbi. This is the title that Jesus was addressed by. He spoke neither Roman nor Greek. He was a Hebrew and He had nothing in common with the casuistics of the Greek or Roman speculators in theology. The great message of Jesus is love to all, neighbor and stranger, friend and foe. This is an old teaching of His old people, only He said it so touchingly and so very profoundly. But the message of the Church Fathers was fire and sword against the whole world of Israel. Jesus lived and perished in a world of Israel; Israel under the boot of the Roman legions but spiritually free, and Jesus was part of this freedom. His sermons spoke of the world within, of infinite kindness, generosity and charity.

Where is the charity in the writings of the fanatical fathers of this fanatical group of churches? It seems they are certain of nothing in their theology except of the hatefulness of the demon Jew. Henry VIII, the adulterous decapitator, founder and head of the Anglican Church, would have no Jews in England. Neither would Queen Isabella in Spain. And Martin Luther would want them only in the slave stables. And of the popes I will not speak more than is necessary. Their own historians refused to hide the truth. There has lately been a lot of talk about a dialogue between Christians and Jews. We don't want to talk to them. We only want them to stop talking against us in their books, in their press, in their speeches, in their sermons, in their homes. We want them to cease playing that dreadful and hateful drama of the crucifixion of a god who did not die.

Perhaps it didn't occur to them that there are among our people still the living sons and daughters of the kin of Jesus. How many of them were killed by the churchgoing Germans of the Hitler era I do not know, but if the kin of Jesus are still living, they attend a synagogue and not a church. And whoever loves Jesus cannot hate His people. And who hates His people is not a Christian.

And no matter how scholarly the early Church Fathers were, from Justin to Augustine, Christians they were not.

V

The Scourge of Rome

Even if the story of Roman crucifixion were not Gospel Truth, even if the Romans would deny having crucified Jesus Christ, they have admittedly and historically killed Christ a thousand times over in the martyrdom of His witnesses. Those who bore witness to Jesus were martyred by the Romans in relentless pursuit for over three hundred years. Why must we therefore even endeavor to assume that they left unmolested and unpunished the *spiritus rector* of all this religious pursuit?

The Jews, on the other hand, were a subject nation in their own land just like the rest of the Mediterranean world. At the time of Jesus, Judea was no more than the southernmost part of the Roman vassal state Syria. No haughty representative of the oppressive Roman authority would accept a command, a judgment or even a suggestion by any of the rebellious Jews. And rebellious they were. Time and time again, they broke out, trying to cast off the yoke of Caesar that burdened their shoulders. And soon after the death of Jesus the Judeans are to be found in widespread rebellion driving the Roman legions across the border. But the unsurpassed military might of Rome came into play. Legion after legion poured into the little land, surrounding its villages and towns in bloody massacre, and finally taking Jerusalem after a siege of two years. And even then it was not the Roman sword but plague and starvation that brought about the destruction of the city and temple of Solomon.

Some historians maintain that all we know of Jesus is that He died a deliberate death at the hand of disbelievers; perhaps we do not know who killed Him, but we do know who believed in Him.

The only ones who believed in Him were the Jews. Not all of them, to be sure, but those who sat at his feet and listened were Jews, and Jews only, and those who carried His message across the world were Jews, and Jews only. The only historian of His time to refer to Him was the Jew Josephus Flavius. The other great historian of this era, who lived more than a hundred years later, the Greek scholar Celsus, considered Jesus a fakir who duped the Jews with Egyptian magic.

Far be it from me to adopt the vindictive Christian attitude of blaming a whole nation for a most unlikely deed perpetrated two thousand years ago under circumstances escaping reality.

We do not wish to turn religious wrath against the Romans of today, although for a thousand years and more the Italian popes, cardinals and bishops strongly emphasized their Roman heritage. But if anyone has to live down a shameful heritage of most unsavory character, it is the Romans. They burned and sacked in bloody conquest Athens and Corinth, Carthage and Syracuse, Alexandria and Jerusalem. If I would want to list all the towns and cities put to blood-sprinkled ashes by the Roman soldateska, I would have to fill all the pages of this little book with nothing but their names.

The Romans of antiquity were the killers in antiquity, and the death of Jesus is just a dot in their horror-drenched history book. They were not satisfied with killing their captives and victims by sword and stone, by hammer and nail—in one month they crucified seven thousand captured followers of Spartacus who rose in a historic fight for freedom—their agents hunted the jungles of Africa for wild animals to devour Christians. And the feeding of lions and tigers with live Christian bodies stopped only when the jungles of the Black Continent had been emptied of the wild beasts.

One can count by the thousands the Christians martyred by the Romans, and the nature of the murders of the believers was far more horrible than that of Jesus on the cross.

That the Christian Church slowly but definitely drifted

47

into the hands of non-Jewish priests and bishops, and that finally the bishop of Rome became *pontifex maximus* at the hands of a Byzantine pagan, that is one of the oddities of European history, which would matter little except that the Roman priests of the Christian churches in all their mutual and most disagreeable quarrels joined in a hate-filled camaraderie against the disbelieving Jews.

But in spite of all the horror they unleashed and the horrible things they perpetrated on the people of the Jewish faith, all the other religions of the Roman Empire fell by the wayside except the mother religion of all monotheism, the Covenant of Israel with God.

VI

The Vicar of Christ

Hatred begins in the heart and not in the head. In so many instances we do not hate people because of a particular deed, but rather do we find that deed ugly because we hate them.

Because of the relentlessly preached antagonism against the Jews as the killers of Christ, the Christian communities throughout the world have always looked upon the Jew with suspicion, distrust and disdain.

They did not permit the Jew to hold public office, to be an officer in their armies, to own any land in his own name, et cetera. I do not wish to bore the reader with the

49

multiple restrictions placed upon Jews throughout the Christian era. I should like to mention at this time that there were laudable exceptions in some communities, in some cities, at certain times, under certain rulers, but exceptions they were indeed. As late as 1914 in Germany, a Jew could not become an officer, although twelve thousand German Jews gave their lives for the Kaiser. As late as 1914, Jews could only live in certain cities of Russia by specially granted privilege from the Czar. As late as the middle of the nineteenth century a Jew could not be elected in England as a member of the House, and even a man of the stature of Disraeli had to become a convert to Christianity in order to fulfill his career.

In what manner the Christians of Germany and Austria turned upon the Jews of Europe requires no description from my poor pen. And for the apologists of those Germans and Austrians I should like to state that innumerable photographs of Christian men and women led by Catholic priests and Protestant ministers are available to those seriously interested, giving irrefutable evidence of the thunderous enthusiasm rendered Hitler and his gang. These pictures show the benign and cheerful countenances of Christian churchmen not only blessing the arms of the murderous Hitler storm-troops, but welcoming them at the Nazi festivals, Nazi-sponsored church affairs, Nazi public gatherings, Nazi receptions, Nazi-sponsored musicals and Nazi-arranged victory celebrations. In fact there is no public event during the Hitler decade in Germany and in Austria in which the Christian churches did not cheerfully participate. The Cardinal of Vienna, Innitzer, during that era signed all his correspondence with "Heil Hitler!" And the Bishop of Rome himself, Pope Pius XII, a former papal nunzio in Berlin, refused even to utter a plea of pity in behalf of one million Jewish children being put to death in airtight trains and gas chambers.

The very same pope, however, did not hesitate at all to raise loud and emphatic protest to President Roosevelt and Prime Minister Churchill against the bombardment of the monastery in Casino by Allied planes. The monastery contained valuable *incunabula* in the basement, and on the roof a Nazi outpost.

The pope maintained coldly in the face of frequent queries from abroad that he wanted to remain neutral and an appeal in behalf of Jews, even Jewish infants, would taint the unblemished neutrality he had been observing.

The very same pope, however, honored numerous leaders of Nazism with lengthy personal interviews, with cordial special blessings, bestowing special honors upon outstanding laymen in the service of Adolf Hitler, the most prominent of whom was von Papen, Hitler's Mephistophelic mentor.

In Hitler's decade there was only one German clergyman, by the name of Lichtenberg, who openly and distinctly branded the killing of Jewish women and children as an unforgivable crime against the Holy Ghost. It is true he died in a concentration camp, but all the other German, Austrian and Italian clergymen who failed to see the bleeding children at their doorstep lived on to praise Jesus. Indeed, if you raise this issue now, as I do and others did before me, these clergymen become rather annoyed with our unwillingness to forget.

For ten years these clergymen spoke in their pulpits in such high voices of the love of Jesus that their whole flock of seventy million German Christians could not hear the whispering of the choking infants and the death outcry of martyred mothers.

So effective was the teaching of hate and contempt for Jewish creatures in the churches and schools of Europe that such unheard of bestiality could go on in front of their very eyes without moving their hate blackened hearts.

If Jesus came back today and set foot on the continent of Europe, He would not kneel at the casket of Pius XII. He would wander on to one of the great German concentration camps where His chained kinsmen were starved to death and their children gassed to death, and He would kneel at their graves and pray—not for them, because if there is a heaven above, that is where they are—but pray for the living and the dead in the black cloth who stood idly by when this savagery occurred and would not speak a word in behalf of the children of Israel.

VII

Crusaders for Christ

The anti-Jewish efforts of the Catholic Church in sermon and legislation reached their height during the centuries of the Crusades. Whatever the motives were of the Church and a subservient, impoverished royalty and aristocracy to set upon the conquest of the wealthy Eastern part of the Mediterranean, the Jews were the immediate sufferers. The story of the crucifixion became the focal point of anti-Jewish and anti-Moslem tirades by fanatical monks and priests. And to the masses of ragged volunteers in the cause of liberating endangered Christian relics from the hands of the Moslems, the immediate opportunity opened itself to fall upon the killers of Christ in their own towns and communities. The Crusades represent one of the great massacres of Jews caused directly by a bloody theology of crucifixion bent on vengeance.

Even on those rulers and subjects not directly involved in the process of crusading expansion, the constant anti-Jewish poison-tongue appears had effect. The feudal lords of Western Europe since the days of Charlemagne were in great need of skilled and learned men whom they could entrust with management, advisory and direct assistance in their economic affairs. One must bear in mind that Charlemagne himself never managed to write more than just his own name, and in the schooling of his knights and the male offspring of the gentlepeople only those arts were obligatory that dealt with fighting, troubadouring, chess and horsemanship.

The Jews were then, as ever, people of the Book. They had a gift for science, civics, commerce and industry. As they had been ruled chattel of the prince from Saint Augustine to Saint Thomas Aquinas, the courts took advantage of this prerogative and often made Jews their personal charge.

As trade in general, and especially that involving seafaring or caravans, was extremely hazardous, subject to wind and weather, and the sea lanes as well as the roads which existed were endangered by pirates and brigands, and many of the knights were dependent upon marauding for part of their supplies and other necessities—the merchants as well as the nobles were compelled to reimburse the lender at a steep interest rate for any sums borrowed.

The borrower had to wait for his ship or caravan to come in to repay his debt, and if ship or caravan failed to reach its destination, the lender could get little satisfaction in placing the borrower in debtors' prison. For that reason, throughout Western Europe, from Sicily to London, the lender demanded and received a "usurious" interest commensurate with the chance he took. He was, in a way, not a banker but a partner to the business.

Even sober historians of the feudal and manorial era have failed to take into proper consideration these particular conditions, and commonly refer to the medieval form of banking as "usury."

Taking as an example England of the Middle Ages, we find that the court and the princes were deeply engaged in the financing of nobles as well as merchants. They were equally concerned with problems of proper taxation upon earnings—townsmen as well as the landowning nobility and high clergy. And it must be said in all fairness that the kings of England did not hesitate on occasion to rob the monasteries, the bishops, the nobles, as well, of course, as the Jews. The Jews, however, they robbed after having made ample use of their particular organizatory and fiscal talents.

On many occasions the kings of England maneuvered to have townsmen, nobles and landowning clergy borrow money from the Jews to pay their taxes and other fees, only to later on denounce the Jews as "usurers." This process of scapegoating we find again and again, even in contemporary history. Some of the kings and princes, such as William II of England or Frederick II of the Holy

Roman Empire, were inclined to protect their learned Jewish advisers and assistants. But the Catholic clergy, as in later centuries the Protestant, insisted on death or expulsion for the killers of Christ.

Even the great codifiers of the Byzantine Empire, Theodosius and Justinian, although subject to the typical Christian Jew-hatred, were far less vindictive in their planning and actions than the ever irate dominant clergy made them be. It was at the time of the coronation of Richard the Lionhearted in 1189 when open wrath against the Jews broke out in England, much to the displeasure of the king, who considered them of great service to his reign. The following year brought about one of the many massacres of the nonbelievers directly caused by raving monks and priests who harangued the townsmen and peasants to annihilate the enemies of Christ. Many of the Jews took their own lives and those of their families in order not to fall into the hands of the bestial clergy.

One must bear in mind that throughout the centuries of the medieval era the Jews were not admitted to any craftsmen's guild, nor were they permitted to acquire farmlands, warehouses or businesses. All they could do was hire themselves out as middlemen to non-Jews. Again and again ecclesiastical curbs were imposed upon them, such as isolation in crowded ghettos, the wearing of a degrading garb, the prohibition of Christians to trade or fraternize with them.

In the year 1262, in London alone fifteen hundred Jews were killed by enraged masses led by cross-bearing clergy. In 1279 all the Jews of London were arrested on trumped-up charges, and 280 were publicly executed. In 1290, under pressure of the Archbishop of Canterbury, Edward I expelled all Jews from England, compelling them, incidentally, to leave all their property to the Crown. Seventeen thousand, the last Jews of England, left for France and Belgium. Many of them, however, never reached the shores of the Continent, being thrown into the sea by the captains for their personal belongings. Not a single priest in all England raised his voice to protest such inhumanity. This was in the year 1290. We have found the same silence among the priests and ministers of 1940. Much in the world has changed in these seven hundred years, but nothing at all in the attitude of Christian clergy against the race of "Christ killers."

The University of Oxford still has a great body of books taken from the expelled Jews.

No Jew was permitted to enter England from 1290, the year of the great suicide, to 1659, when Oliver Cromwell, acting upon an appeal by Rabbi Menasse Ben Israel, authorized re-entry of persons of the Jewish faith.

One of the most horrid aspects of church-dominated medieval England was the deliberate and demoniacal planting of ritual murder stories among the peasantry and the townsfolk. This type of propaganda was so successfully put forth by the clergy that in the thirteenth century the churchgoing masses suspected every Jew of crucifying children on high holidays. When in the year 1255 a Christian boy of 8, known as Hugh of Lincoln, was found in a well, scores of Jews were apprehended, of whom eighteen were executed, and under torture they all had confessed to having taken part in the crucifixion of the boy. Such was the atmosphere of that time that the widely known Catholic Duns Scotus, *doctor subtilis,* earnestly suggested that all children be taken from the Jews and baptized by force, and that those parents who refused to bow to the will of Christ be transported to a penal island. In the year 1282 the Archbishop of Canterbury closed all synagogues in his diocese. Six years before, in Norwich, a Jew was burned alive for refusing to admit that Jesus was God.

Any Christian who met his death in the anti-Jewish pogroms that the flaming Crusades brought about was considered a martyr. At the Stamford massacres, a ghoulish peasant caught plundering Jewish victims was killed in a knifing by another plunderer. He was canonized by request of the Bishop of Lincoln. This brought a great influx of reverential people to the town, as his corpse was said to be performing great miracles. In fact, this desire for pilgrims may have been at the bottom of quite a number of the ritual murder legends.

The fanatical crusading clergy ran wild not only in England, they were equally vehement on the Continent. "God wills it," was the slogan that came from the lips of monks and priests in white fury, encouraging the crusader riffraff of hordes of disorganized mobs of beggar knights, bankrupt nobles, animalistic serfs and illiterate monks to kill the infidels at home. In the city of Rouen in France, every Jew who did not accept baptism was put to death. One of the most ferocious of the anti-Semitic clergy was the infamous Peter the Hermit, a priest of Amiens. Only his death in 1151 stopped his venomous tongue. In the

German city of Worms very few of the Jews escaped the wrath of the Crusaders. The same happened in the city of Mainz, where the bishop participated in the division of spoils of the "Christ killers." In the city of Ratisbon in Germany, all the Jewish citizens were driven to the Danube. Those who refused baptism in the blue waters were drowned in them. In the year 1099, when the first Crusaders finally took Jerusalem, they assembled all the Jews in the great synagogue and burned them alive, and while the temple was ablaze they marched around it singing "Christ We Adore Thee."

Again, I should like to emphasize that some of the worldly rulers of Germany and France, like Henry IV (1056-1106), were disturbed by these outrages, and in some cases even attempted to bring culprits to justice and to permit convert Jews to return to their true faith. But the Catholic clergy was too powerful to be obstructed, and the tale of crucifixion was deeply embedded in the heart of every Christian man, woman and child. They wouldn't kill a chicken the way they murdered Jews, and the delight they expressed in these massacres, as narrated by numerous chroniclers, they certainly would not have had at the burning of a squeaking animal.

In a thousand years the Church had done its job well. Killing a Jew, torturing a Jew, was Christian virtue, and the suffering of a Jew, even a Jewish child, was an act of divine justice exacted upon the crucifiers of the Lord Himself.

VIII

Pogroms and the Cross

The high priest of early Christian anti-Semitism was Saint John Chrysostom (344-407), patriarch of Constantinople, by far the most influential preacher of his time, referred to as "the bishop with the golden tongue." Here is some of the rhetoric from that golden tongue:

> "The Jews are the most worthless of all men— they are lecherous, greedy, rapacious—they are perfidious murderers of Christians, they worship the devil, their religion is a sickness—"

The gentle saint goes on:

"The Jews are the odious assassins of Christ and for killing God there is no expiation possible, no indulgence or pardon. Christians may never cease vengeance, and the Jews must live in servitude forever. God always hated the Jews, and whoever has intercourse with Jews will be rejected on Judgment Day. It is incumbent upon all Christians to hate the Jews."

Thus read the homilies of the foremost orator of early Catholicism. Regretfully, he differs only in coarseness of expression and bluntness of animosity from the other early Church Fathers.

These men, imbued with a fierce and merciless hatred against the Jews, intertwined their theology and their historiography with demonological craftsmanship, the result of which was the flame-breathing dragon of anti-Semitism.

With such vile and monstrous accusations supported by an allegedly divine scholarship, reinforced in sanctifications and canonizations, shouted by every monk and every priest from every pulpit in every church and by church-appointed teachers in every classroom of every school, is it then surprising that nobles, as well as common townsmen, merchants as well as serfs, in all the cities and hamlets of Christian Europe, looked upon the Jew as an abomination, a living replica of the devil himself, lurking in the background to do evil to the followers of Christ?

In Germany when the Black Plague of the fourteenth century hit the nation, the issue was not to find out what brought about the Black Death. With the last sermon still ringing in their ears, the issue was quickly resolved into a denunciation of the Jewish devils, and under the torture of rack and flame scores of them confessed they had poisoned the wells, as they had confessed in this and other countries that they had crucified children on holy days, as they confessed they had desecrated the consecrated wafers containing the body of Christ. There is nothing people will not admit to when white-hot tongs probe at their breasts or genitals. In over two hundred communities of Germany, Jewish inhabitants were put to the indescribable tortures of which the Catholic Church was such a subtle master, and finally put to death. In Freiburg six hundred were burned at the stake. In Strassburg all two thousand were dispatched.

Some of the worldly rulers of Germany as well as France made halfhearted efforts to stop this medieval holocaust, which finds its counterpart only in the Hitler massacre. But the souls of the citizenry had been blackened by church-promulgated anti-Semitism. A single German, by the name of Rindfleisch, was able in the late thirteenth century to surround himself with mobs of people roving from town to town in Germany and Austria, wherever he went making bonfires of the living bodies of Jewish children, women and unarmed men.

In the declining century of the medieval ages, after fifteen hundred years of Christian teachings and practice, we find the Jewish people of Europe decimated, nay, much more than that, cut in half by the fury of commoners and nobles alike, expelled from England, France and Spain, most evilly dealt with in Germany, scurrying for refuge to the far north and east, to the Slavic countries where some gentle ruler like Casimir the Great of Poland had opened the gates of his country; fleeing to the haven of Turkey and other Moslem countries, any pagan country that was out of the reach of the pen, the tongue and the sword of the Christian church leaders.

The barbaric Slavs, the barbaric Moslems, and the barbaric pagans saved the Jews from total extinction.

A distinguished statistician of history has estimated that the total population of Jews in the year 1940 would have been over 100 million—it would have been the greatest nation in the Western world, had it not been for the incessant massacres and forceful conversions by its Christian oppressors.

The network of anti-Semitic Catholic laws was systematized by the fourth Lateran Council in 1215, convoked by the infamous Pope Innocent III. These laws were intensified as the centuries went on by successive papal Bulls.

So unbearable was the yoke of the Jew in the Christian world that even the nagging rigors of life in the papal possessions appeared tolerable in comparison with the harassment and malevolence outside of them.

Some people ask, in connection with the various anti-Semitic waves of the centuries, such as the Crusades, the Inquisition, the ritual murderer charges, the plague accusations, the Cossack pogroms in seventeenth-century Poland, and finally the hell of Hitlerism, "How come the Christian churches failed to speak up and failed to act?"

This is no more than a rhetorical question. The churches did speak up and the churches did act. Unfortunately so for two thousand years. They spoke of the Jew as the killer of God, and they spoke of the Jew as the forever accursed hereditary deicide criminal.

If the Church Fathers had not spoken as they did, and the popes and bishops had not acted as they did, none of this carnage would have occurred.

The Christian church put the seed of hate into the hearts of its people, and from that dragon seed grew the monsters, from Chrysostom to Hitler and from Torquemada to Chmielnicki. Even in centuries when Jews were totally absent from certain countries, divines of the church continued to preach Jew hatred, in their daily catechisms, in their sermons, in their essays, even in their prayers and hymns.

They had to have someone to hate, and the way the Church Fathers had pictured the Jew, he was it. They put horns on the Jew's head, and the great Michelangelo did not hesitate to uglify his magnificent Moses with a pair of horns.

The Jew was the devil's son, the crucifier of the living God, and punishing him, as Saint Chrysostom said, was the duty of every Christian, and that is one duty they rarely neglected.

In seventeenth-century France, which was *Judenrein* as can be, the renowned clergyman Jacques Bénigne Bossuet made this appeal to the Christians of both the Catholic and Protestant denomination:

"The Jews are monsters, hated universally.
They are beggars and the butt of the world's jokes.

Thus has the Lord punished them for killing His Son."

This type of sermonizing went on for hundreds of years in Spain, in France, in England, and of course in Germany, even during those many centuries when no Jew was to be found within their borders. When Oliver Cromwell in the year 1659 readmitted the Jews to England, he had to do so by a ruse, because the English clergy refused to share their island with the crucifiers.

Martin Luther took at face value the vilest accusations against the Jews. In his *Schem Hamphoras,* Luther referred to the Jews as ritual murderers, poisoners of wells, and being worse than devils, demanded destruction of all their synagogues and Talmuds. Hitlerism was a logical outcome of Lutheranism, just as the Crusades' massacres were a logical outcome of anti-Semitic Vaticanism. What can we expect of adherents to a church, the pope of which (Paul IV, 1555) allowed Jews only as servants, compelling them to wear a yellow badge, restricting them to a ghetto existence without permission to speak to a Christian. This very same pope was responsible for the burning of sixty Marranos, whom he accused of reverting to Judaism. With popes like Paul IV and Protestants like Martin Luther, what hope for the people of Israel?

The Greek Orthodox Church and the other Eastern churches drew their attitudes toward the Jews from the very same early Church Fathers, and they are as responsible for inciting and activating anti-Semitism in the land of the Czar as the Catholic Church in Poland was guilty of undermining the position of the Jews who had fled Western Europe.

To some, the Roman cross is a symbol of charity, of supreme love and devotion. To the Jew it is a reminder of perennial persecution. The cross to the Jew is the symbol of pogrom.

The *Junta Suprema* of the Inquisition watched the agonies of their victims under the sign of the cross; the early Church Fathers laid the cross over their chest when they spoke of the Jews; the Crusaders carried the cross on their banners, on their tunics, on their shields; and every one of the fascist executioners had some kind of cross or another on his uniform; even the miserable Jewish victims being marched to the stake had a cross painted on their Inquisition hats.

Throughout these two thousand years, during which the Christian churches practiced the teaching and preaching of hateful contempt against the Jew as the devil crucifier, the cross stood always cold and condemning in front of its Jewish victims. To the Jew the cross is the sign of hate and condemnation.

As the Middle Ages reached their end, with the Renaissance and its accompanying widespread education and intellectual interaction, large groups of individuals obtained access to true facts and true history; for the Jews a new era began.

Already during the Renaissance great humanists like Montaigne, Mirandola, Erasmus, and Reuchlin raised their voices for a re-evaluation of Judaism and the Jews.

The great march of humanism had begun. In steady though halting steps, men of reason and men of justice marched forward in ever rising number; by the eighteenth century, Europe and the new America were strong enough to wrest the power of government from church and royalty. The march of freedom, the march of enlightenment, the march of personal and social justice, could no longer be stopped.

Men like Rousseau, Locke and Jefferson, and a thousand others too numerous to mention, had won out against the dark forces of reaction and one of its worst aspects, blatant anti-Semitism. The power of the Vatican was broken once and forever, and with it fell the gates of the ghettos, and the yellow spot on the cloak of the Jew.

But the fight for enlightenment is far from over, certainly not as far as the Jew is concerned. The catechisms and the prayerbooks as well as the sermons and the hymns of the Christian priests and ministers still engage in the game of making the Jew a scapegoat in their theology. But there is a light in this still darkness. Some few years ago the voice of John XXIII, one of the few great popes indeed, made itself heard, confessing in all humility, so well becoming this upstanding vicar, that it is wrong to accuse the Jews of deicide;—though the Romans put Him to death, the whole world denied Him and the whole world rejected Him, and it is for the whole world that He wished to die, He, their Redeemer.

So spoke a true man of God.

Will the Christian churches, will the bishops, priests and ministers listen to the admonition of this divine, or will they prefer the olden ways of living by hate and preaching hate of Christ's own people of Israel?

IX

Diaspora

The "dispersion" of the Jews shortly after the death of Christ was used by early Christian apologists and, of course, by the Church Fathers as irrefutable evidence of the guilt of the people of Israel. It can readily be understood that some of the naïve and ignorant first-century chroniclers would seriously believe that the conquest of Jerusalem by the pagans Vespasian and Titus was God's striking the Jews in retaliation for the murder of His Son.

The latter-day theological historians and essayists of the Church would, of course, make extensive use of this superstitious and erroneous interpretation.

The anti-Jewish apologists of the Catholic Church proclaimed in loud and vindictive terms that the Lord had smitten the Jews for the crime of crucifixion and dispersed them all over the world. In *The City of God,* Saint Augustine philosophizes, "The Jews slew Christ and were therefore slain by the Romans and dispersed over the face of the earth." Pope Gregory I (540-604), the spiritual fountainhead of medieval Catholicism, wrote in similar terms, "The apostles of the Crucified had barely reached exile when Titus took Judea and scattered its people into the four corners." Even contemporary theologians, Catholic as well as Protestant, repeat the unhistoric "dispersion" of the Jews as evidence of their guilt of the crucifixion and, of course, as evidence of the wrath of God over the killing of God.

This alleged dispersion of the Jews, together with the alleged condemnation of Christ by the Jews to crucifixion, is used by Christian essayists, historians, preachers, and teachers with unsavory vindictiveness against the Jewish people. The Christian catechisms and textbooks, their sermons and even their novels are full of this blind accusation and shallow historic "proof."

We can forgive the early naïve chroniclers, we can forgive the overzealous Church Fathers, many of whom suffered similar fate as Jesus did from the Roman authorities. A few of these witnesses to the "guilt" of the Jews shared the fate of Jesus at the hands of the Romans. The Romans killed Christ a thousand times in His followers; still some of these very same followers never changed their views about the crucifixion.

We can forgive the naïve and the ignorant, but we cannot forgive the modern Christian theologians and historians for deliberately ignoring the overwhelming archaeological and literary evidence which contradicts the wishful conclusions of the early Church zealots.

For many hundreds of years the Jews had lived in large numbers outside of the Holy Land. When the kingdom of Israel was ravaged in the year 722 B.C. by the Assyrian Sargon and the kingdom of Judah by the Chaldean Nebuchadnezzar in 586 B.C., hundreds of thousands of the Hebrews were either dispersed or taken into captivity into Mesopotamia, Egypt, Arabia and other lands. Indeed, when the Persian conqueror Cyrus permitted the exiled Jews to return to their homeland, the majority of the Babylonian Jews declined to do so.

Josephus Flavius claims that if the Babylonian Jews five hundred years after their captivity had not refused to help their kinsmen in the beleaguered Jerusalem, the legions of Titus would have been cut off and destroyed.

Emigration of Jews into the city of Damascus and into the northern plains of Egypt since the eighth century B.C. is a widely known and substantiated fact. The Egyptians as well as the Syrians used Judeans for centuries before Christ as borderland settlers, civil servants and mercenaries in their armies. The Egyptian rulers of the Pharaonic as well as Hellenistic eras on more than one occasion placed Jewish commanders in charge of their troops.

Where Jews were taken prisoner, as in the case of the Roman conquest, and sold as slaves, they invariably managed by industry and learning to gain their freedom and thus create or enlarge Jewish communities. We find Jewish soldiers already in the armies of Xerxes. The city of Alexandria, founded by the irrepressible conqueror, rapidly drew Jewish immigrants and soon became in Jewish population and culture a rival of Babylon and Jerusalem.

For hundreds of years before the death of Christ we find considerable, even large, Jewish communities in Cyrenaica, in Carthage, in Rome, in Athens, in Syracuse, in Macedonia, in the Iberian Islands, in Ethiopia, even in the mountains of the Caucasus. To speak of the "dispersion" of the Jews in the year 70 is to ignore all historic and archaeological fact. To see in the sacking of Jerusalem by Titus a divine act is sheer blasphemy. If God wanted to punish the Jews He would not have sent the pagan butcher Titus as His avenging angel.

I hate to see a Caesarean monster who had his own statue placed at the altar of all Roman temples deemed by the Christians as acting as the right hand of the Lord.

Only a hundred years after this so-called "dispersion" of the Jews from the Holy Land, the Judeans rose again against the Caesars, this time against Hadrian, and from the year 132 to the year 135 Palestine was a battlefield of those who refused to bow to the yoke of the oppressor. Their leader Bar Kochba was, like Jesus, proclaimed the Messiah, believed by some and not by others, and he too was killed by Roman soldiers. Half a million Jews fell in this war, the last great uprising against Roman sovereignty.

An immense amount of archaeological evidence, including letters by Bar Kochba, has been unearthed in recent years in Israel, giving final evidence to counter the ridiculous anti-Semitic tale of the dispersion of the Jews as punishment for the crucifixion of Jesus. No one who wishes for the truth can deny this evidence. And history has no power to convince those who desire malicious tradition to retain its foothold. The purposeful agitator has little interest in either facts or opinions that cross his aims.

May I add at this time in connection with this "dispersion" that the great canonical literature of Israel, the many volumed books of the Talmud, the Mishna and the Gamara, the Midrash and the Kabbala, all were created after the death of Jesus in the Holy Land and, in part, in Babylon. In fact, the writers of the Babylonian as well as the Jerusalem Talmud communicated within both these lands, and while the Kabbala reached deep into the golden era of Spanish Jewry, it too had its origin in Palestine.

The flowering of Jewish religious thought came after the death of Jesus, and that is perhaps the reason why the Christian emperor Justinian placed the Talmud on the "prohibited" list. The prohibition of the Talmud in the sixth century undoubtedly set a precedent for the medieval burnings of these books so strongly advocated by both the Vatican as well as its archenemy, Martin Luther.

An indication of the numerical and social importance of the Jews in the post-Jesus era of Palestine is shown in the position of the Ethnarch or Patriarch who represented to the Roman authorities the local ruler of the Jews. The Romans recognized the Jewish head as the religious and social leader of his people. After the Christianization of the Byzantine Empire, the Jews were subjected to incessant discrimination and violence at the hands of the Christian authorities.

Peace came to the Jews in the Middle East as well as in North Africa with the rule of the Moslems, only, as far as Palestine is concerned, to be obliterated by the Crusaders. In the year 1099 the bearers of the cross drove the last Jews of Jerusalem into the synagogue and put the edifice to the torch. After that year, and as long as the Christians ruled the territory, no Jew was to be found aboveground in the Holy Land.

X

What's Wrong with the Christians?

The idea of the Jew as a killer of God and in punishment thereof a member of a race forever on the run is so deeply ingrained in the minds of persons raised in the Christian faith that even a man like Pascal, the French Catholic theologian and scientist, considered their miserable fate a just punishment.

If a man like Pascal could look upon the merciless persecution of the Jews by his Christian contemporaries with phlegmatic self-righteousness, what can we expect of the great masses of Christians who lack the capacity to rethink fundamentals? We have seen what the Christians have done to the Jews since the days of the early Church Fathers. We find there, as we find throughout Western history, an incessant stream of accusations against the Jews, beginning with the original allegations of the murder of God, who wanted to die as a Redeemer, and following this prejudgment, we find widespread Christian satisfaction with an alleged sudden dispersion of the Jews throughout the world as divine punishment.

This in spite of the simple historic fact known even to the semiliterate that not the Jews but the Romans were the killers of the Christians for three hundred years, and that there is not the slightest evidence that the Jews were in the habit of killing self-proclaimed Anointed Ones, or even renegades, and that the apostles, as well as Saint Paul and other Christian converts, appeared time and time again before the Kehilah in the synagogues trying to interpret the Messiah the way they saw Him.

But once it obtained ecclesiastic power over the Roman Empire the Catholic Church desired to break the stubborn neck of the only people who refused to accept the dominant religion. The inflexible Jews refused to bend before the cross as they had refused to bend before the image of Caesar. Caesar forgave them their vague monotheism. The Bishop of Rome would not. Neither would his clergy, high or low.

As the Roman Empire was still bound in considerable traditional legalism, the bishops could only rant and rave against the Jews, deface and even burn their synagogues, admonish their followers to have no dealings with Jews. But they had no power to kill them. Indeed, they rarely did.

What's Wrong with the Christians?

As a rule they would incite the mobs to do the burning and killing, and when the heat of destruction was over and the bodies were cold, these bishops and their priests would fall into a deadly silence, interrupted only by occasional shrieks of vituperation trying to justify the claim of original sin of the Jews and their ignominy of disbelief in Christ.

The present Pope, Paul VI, said once, "The love that Christ brought into the world is not yet in the hearts of men." No truer sentence was ever spoken. But if in two thousand years the Christians have not learned the Hebraic wisdom of love of man, will they ever? If the early Church Fathers ranted against the Jews like creatures out of hell, are we to assume that the cathedra theologians of today are of a more lofty disposition?

I don't think they have anything to add to the irrefutable crimson lessons they have given us, and the last generation saw a culmination of Christian teachings to the Jews, when a million of our children were brutally brought to death by the most churchgoing nation of Europe; when suddenly the bishops, the priests and the ministers fell into deadly silence and the Vicar of Christ himself decided to be "neutral." Neutral, in the war of ten million German soldiers, whose weapons his church blessed time and time again, against a million infants.

What admirable sense of judicial objectivity. It reminds one of the medieval disputations arranged by royal order between rabbis and priests, where the priests had the privilege of total abuse while the rabbis had in front of them the threat of the cross and the threat of the gallows.

We don't need any dialogue with the Christians. The

best they have to offer they have demonstrated in two thousand years of abuse and persecution. All we ask them is to cease maligning us in print and in the spoken word, to tear out of their school books the vicious, malevolent fabrication of the Jews as killers of God. The Jews, who have given them God. If not for the Jews, they would still be sacrificing virgins to their Olympic and Teutonic idols. We ask them to tear out from their catechisms the monstrous Golgotha accusations of a cunning and vicious clergy of the Dark Ages; to cease teaching the falsehood of a Jewish diaspora under Titus as punishment for their sins. More Jews lived in Babylon at the time of the crucifixion than in any city of Palestine outside of Jerusalem, and more Jews lived in Alexandria than in Babylon. At the time of Christ every fifth person in the Mediterranean basin was a Semite.

What became of the many Sons of Israel who were the dread of the Roman Emperors? The history of Christianity is the story of merciless persecution, degradation and annihilation of Christ's people.

We ask you to take out of your prayer books and your hymns the venomous slander against our people. Can't you even pray or sing to your God without humiliating the ones He loved so much?

Is there a crime your clergymen have not accused the Jews of? When pestilence stalked your filthy streets, you pointed a finger at the Jews. When your wells were contaminated by your sewage, your monks whispered about Jewish witchcraft. When a vagabond found a dead child, your deacons remembered the ancient "saints," claiming, "The Jews need blood for their holy days, Christian blood." When your rulers used the Jewish skill to tax the people, your churches pointed to the Talmud. When your nobles used the diligence of Jewish supervisors and agricultural planners, it was easy to turn the serfs and villeins on the "sons of the devil." There is no crime you failed to accuse the Jews of, and even where no crime was committed and there were no Jews in the land, there was still the old accusation of Christ on the cross to keep the Christian faith alert and inspired.

Nothing is so infectious as hate, nothing is so easy to impart as hate, and in two thousand years you managed, to the glory of God, to keep the flames of hate against the Jews burning.

Every Christian minister in this country and abroad who brings the Gospel version of the death of Christ as it is written and authorized by the Jew-hating Roman bishops of the fourth century is a teacher of hate and contempt against *am olam*, the eternal people, as Saint Paul called them.

Until such day as you have ceased to consider revelation what is only bias and perjury, we must look upon those who are in the service of the Christian religion not as being out to bind mankind together, which is the meaning of the word *religio*, but to separate it.

This little book is not in the form of a dialogue. You have nothing to tell us that you have not said already, and most cruelly so. This is a monologue of one Jew out of little more than ten million.

Ever since your era began, you have given us death and devastation. In Seville your bishops had horses drag us to the scaffold, and our three synagogues were turned into churches. The edifices are still there, but no trace of the bones. They were all burned. In Toledo you threw us off the cliff and our two great synagogues were turned into cathedrals. The edifices are still there.

Is there a city in Europe or in the Middle East where no pyres have consumed our bones? London and York, Madrid and Valencia, Paris and Poitiers, Mainz and Vienna, Warsaw and Kielce, Kiev and Jassi, Rome and Jerusalem.

There is no city within your domain that has not witnessed the bestiality of your anti-Semitism. And at the base of it all, in the final analysis, was and is the evil legend concocted by scheming Roman fanatics.

Is your faith so weak, is your devotion so poor that you must have the Jewish hate story as part of your theological structure?

Can you have no Gospel without gall, and no redemption without condemning the Jews, like Prometheus, to have their livers hacked at every day by the vultures of fanaticism?

Not a Sunday goes by without your lesson in hate and contempt against the people of Israel. You repeat the words of Jesus the Hebrew, of love to your enemies, but you can't even love His own people, His own family, His own folk with whom He lived. They are among us, not among you, those of them who are still alive and who escaped becoming victims of your theology in action.

Can't you worship Jesus without disparaging the Jews? Can't you adore Mary without condemning her father and her mother? Can't you admire Saint Paul without abusing his family and friends?

Can't you love without hate? And if you must hate the Jews of today for a guilt that isn't theirs, you must hate the ancient peoples, from King David on and before, because they gave life to the people you say murdered God. But it is this King David whom you take pains in listing as the ancestral father of Jesus.

No religion except the Christian has interwoven into its theology so gruesome a chapter as that called the Jewish crime of crucifixion. Neither Buddhism nor Hinduism, Confucianism nor Taoism, Mohammedanism nor Shintoism, no faith in the world in historic times has such a horrible scheme of revulsive hate integrated into its very tenets of belief.

It seems Christianity cannot tell its story without a tale of hate, and this tiny but cutting tale has put uncounted millions to a torturous death and many more to a life of undeserved humiliation and suffering. And this tiny vicious tale will keep on having its toll of destruction unless those who truly believe in Christ have a dialogue with their better selves and make an end to this bitter figment.

XI

What's Wrong with the Jews?

The last twenty years have seen a remarkable change at least in the external manifestations of Christian theologians. The stunning events of the Hitler era convinced even the dullest that there must be something wrong in Christian religious education that could make possible such a collusion of churchgoing Christians, the majority of whom, of course, were Germans, to choke to death millions of innocent and unarmed civilians.

The second blow hit these theologians when they had to realize that the overwhelming majority of churchgoers, the German ones in particular, have little guilt feeling, but rather are concerned with going on as if nothing had happened. Indeed, to the ordinary European of the non-Jewish race World War II was just another military conflict with its usual destruction of life and property. To judge by the war record of the Hitler armies, they behaved in the occupied territories not much different than other armies did. By and large the American, British and French prisoners of war returned to their homes unscathed, and as far as the Russians were concerned in their relationship to the German prisoners, they treated each other with equal indolence.

Although some German non-Jews were placed in concentration camps, even the majority of the Communists among them came out alive. The only mass victims of Hitler's unheard-of brutality were the Jews. The few hundred thousand whose fate was yet "unsolved" in the final solution were mere skin and bone, on the verge of expiring, living among lifeless skeletons of cellmates.

Most of the Christian theologians, except the right wing of the Catholic curia under the leadership of the Bishop Luigi Carli, felt something had to be done in the direction of a "reconciliation" with the Jews. The right wing of the Catholic Church, however, expressed its agreement with the still dominant theorem of Bishop Carli that according to the tradition of the Catholic Church the Jews are responsible for the crucifixion of Christ, for which they have justly been accursed by God, and the events of the past only prove their abomination.

I will admit that the majority of the Catholic clergy is not entirely disposed to seeing an act of God in the acts of

Hitler and his storm troopers, although during the Hitler decade people like the Viennese Cardinal Innitzer and the devout Julius Streicher made it a point to identify the Jew-destroying goal of National Socialism with the many anti-Semitic pronouncements of Catholic and Protestant theologians.

So powerful is the right wing of the Catholic Church that until this writing it has been impossible for the recently convening council to pass a declaration absolving the living Jews from responsibility in the alleged crucifixion in the town of Jerusalem two thousand years ago. This whole situation is most embarrassing to the enlightened Catholic clergy in America, as the violent anti-Semitism of the ancestral Christian theologians is reprehensible to all liberal clergy.

Embarrassment alone will help little in this situation. Throughout history there were embarrassed ministers and priests; a few of them paid with their lives for trying to stop anti-Semitic pogroms. But until the great body of Christian clergy has obtained insight into the evil aspects of their theology, anti-Semitism will remain a major aspect of the Western world.

The crucifixion of the Jew Jesus by order of the whole Jewish community has been made a cornerstone of all Christian theology, supported by the implication that in the eyes of God the Jews are forever accursed, and that every Jewish child in your town, and every Jewish woman in your town, and every man, is a congenital sinner and criminal.

This whole hate-born structure of religious malevolence,

fabricated by incensed Roman bishops and philosophically elaborated by a group of revenge-eager Church Fathers, even today dominates all denominations under the cross.

Indeed, the cross and the crucifix are a constant reminder of the deviltry of the Jews, the "God-hated" killers of His Son.

No matter how much or little the average Christian knows about the theology of his particular church, of one aspect even the most ignorant or indifferent among them will never be unaware: the Jews and the crucifixion. Buddha once preached: "In the innermost of the Eternal there is no desire for revenge."

But the Christian does not read Buddha, and his God is an amazingly vengeful one, a God who not only hates a son for the sin of his father, but an infant for a failing that allegedly occurred two thousand years ago. To the Jew it almost appears that all the Christian believers get out of their religion is contempt and hate for the Jew.

It is the only religion that has made the gallows a symbol of love. How can a Christian ever love a Jew if he forever lives in the sight of the gallows? There are many other symbols in Christianity far more beautiful than the cross. The fish, for instance, symbolizing Jesus as the great fisherman of souls.

Some Christian theologians argue that it isn't proper to change the basic tenets of theology. But is it proper to carry on such a basic tenet as the false accusation of deicide on the part of the Jews, leading century after century to indescribable carnage among Christ's own people? Does the modern Christian child or adult have to be told again and again this ugly legend of execution?

The issue is simply this: can Catholicism and Protestantism, east and west, exist by the sheer majesty of the teachings of Jesus, the gentle Jew of Nazareth, or must they have the bloody legend involving the guilt of every Jewish soul, past, living and yet to be born?

Can Christianity exist giving inspiration to a bewildered mankind without at the same time imbuing their minds with raging anti-Semitism?

You cannot teach the present version of the Gospel story, with all its anti-Jewish tendencies, without putting the seed of Jew hatred into the hearts of the readers or listeners, and that is certain. Thousands of years of history have proven it in every generation. The earth of Europe is filled with the Jewish victims of Christian hate. The Germans of the Second World War were only one incident in the century-deep history of anti-Semitism.

All the multiple poison flowers come back to the same seed, Christian religious anti-Semitism. The Christian child drinks its Jew hatred in the mother church. This early impact of the gruesome crucifixion tale is never forgotten.

In this great and blessed country, separation of church and state has prevented overt acts such as pogroms, but those who are keen observers will note on many occasions that even here the seed of hate is not entirely lost though almost entirely suppressed.

The child that grows up in the guidance of Christian teachings will form its own peculiar image of the "Christ killers." It will endow such image with all the attributes of an enemy: an ugly face, an ungainly body, an evil odor. We have innumerable drawings and descriptions from the days of Origen to Streicher and Goebbels demonstrating how Christian youth and Christian adults have visualized the Jew.

Naturally, these pictures are imaginings of hate, and when you hate someone even his blessings appear accursed. It is a truism that in those we hate we see our own faults exaggerated, and that we are envious of anything good, pleasant or beautiful that we find in the hated, and endeavor to minimize or downgrade it. We find an ugly motive in any good thing they do, and any wrong in them we exaggerate immensely.

The early Church Fathers and the early Roman bishops, in order to break the stoutness and stubbornness of the Jewish faith, accused its adherents of every crime, lechery and evil deed that their sick imagination could envision, from the crucifixion of Christian children on Jewish holidays to urinating on consecrated bread taken from a church. Some of these accusations were so vile that I wish to spare the reader their description.

And this vitriolic, merciless and most cruel flame of accusations against the Jews is part of the very fundament of Christian religious education. And again, even these old irascible men of sanctity were outdone in anti-Semitic vindictiveness by Martin Luther.

As a hint of warning, we find during the last two hundred years a certain type of anti-Semitism that appears entirely detached from the theological variety propagated by the

Christian churches. But such appearance is deceiving. It only proves that even if persons have lost faith in the great body of Christian teachings, one thing remains with them, the grim part concerning "Jewish perfidy." They no longer believe in Jesus, they may not even any longer believe in God, but they do believe the Jews to be a nefarious people. They don't really know why they so believe. It is basically emotional, going back to early childhood impressions in church, school and home, and so their active minds searching for justification for this dumb feeling of hate will naturally not look inside their own bleak hearts but seek outside among the Jews of the day or the Jews of hearsay.

If these men are libertines, they will call the Jews perverted and quickly they will find an example of one kind or another to confirm this conviction. If they are radicals, they will discern in the Jew a greedy capitalist. If they themselves are engaged in business, they will find the Jew a financial octopus trying to deprive the honest Christian businessman of fair opportunity. If they are frustrated in their career, they will say the Jew is pushy. They will say the same or worse if they are unsuccessfully engaged in the arts. And if they have nothing else to say, they will proclaim the Jew a member of an inferior race. As they are no longer believing Christians, it wouldn't bother them that Jesus came from the womb of a Jewish woman.

Anti-Semitism, although born in early religious education, can grow to full bloom long after all religious interests have disappeared from the mind of the so-called "social anti-Semite."

There are also "political anti-Semites" who cleverly make

use of the dormant anti-Jewish tendencies in most Christians. They will accuse the Jews of aiming for exactly that particular political power or position they themselves are fighting for.

The bias against the Jew is, like all bias and prejudice, born not in the mind but in the heart. And tragically enough, the hatred of the Jew is born in the alleged devotional service for Jesus, Son of Israel, who gave His life to redeem the world out of hate and envy into the glory of charity. He hoped that all of Israel would stream toward Him in His hour of agony. It is for the people of Israel He prayed, He suffered and died. In His own words, "I did not come to destroy the Torah, but to fulfill it."

The Romans put Him to death as they put to death for three hundred years many thousands of those who stood witness for Him. Yet out of this solemn happening on the soil and among the people of Israel it isn't the killing of the Jew Jesus that is paramount. Many of our own people have died in more gruesome a manner and for neither earthly nor heavenly reason. Many saintly men have died of all faiths. But what has become of all this great tragedy of a nation and its prophet? An evil, insidious teaching of hate and contempt for the very people, the only people, to whom Jesus addressed Himself.

It almost seems, as far as we Jews are concerned, that all the sermons of Jesus were spoken in the wind and what remained were the Roman teachings of hate, still poisoning the world for us by word, by pen and by deed.

Brief Bibliography

Abrahams, I., editor. *The Legacy of Israel.*

Addison, C. A. *The Knights Templars.*

Baum, Gregory. *The Jews and the Gospel.*

Bell, H. Idris. *Cults and Creeds in Graeco-Roman Egypt.*

Berdyaev, Nicolas. *Christianity and Anti-Semitism.*

Bloy, Léon. *Le salut par les juifs.*

Diem, Hermann. *Das Raetsel des Antisemitismus.*

Dubnow, S. M. *History of the Jews in Russia and Poland.*

Eckhardt, A. Roy. *Christianity and the Children of Israel.*

Flannery, Edward H. *The Anguish of the Jews.*

Graetz, Heinrich. *Geschichte der Juden.*

Isaac, Jules. *Genèse de l'Antisémitisme.*

— — —. *The Teaching of Contempt.*

Journet, Charles. *The Church of the Word Incarnate.*

Kerr, William Shaw. *Handbook of the Papacy.*

Knight, G. A. F., editor. *Jews and Christians.*

Kuhner, Hans. *Encyclopedia of the Papacy.*

Lewy, Guenter. *The Catholic Church and Nazi Germany.*

Munck, J. *Christus und Israel.*

Olson, Bernhard E. *Faith and Prejudice.*

Parkes, James. *The Foundations of Judaism and Christianity.*

Poliakow, L. *Du Christ aux juifs de cour.*

Raisin, J. S. *Gentile Reactions to Jewish Ideals.*

Roth, Cecil. *History of the Marranos.*

Runes, Dagobert D. *Despotism: Pictorial History of Tyranny.*

— — —. *The Hebrew Impact on Western Civilization.*

Schuerer, Emil. *A History of the Jewish People in the Time of Jesus Christ.*

Simmel, Ernst. *Anti-Semitism: A Social Disease.*

Sloan, William Wilson. *A Survey of the New Testament.*

Tillich, Paul. *Theology of Culture.*